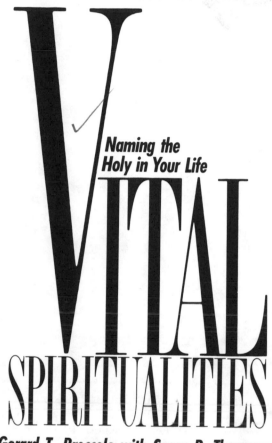

*Naming the
Holy in Your Life*

VITAL
SPIRITUALITIES

Gerard T. Broccolo with Susan B. Thompson

AVE MARIA PRESS   Notre Dame, Indiana 46556

To my parents, John and Rae,
who taught me the basics of spirituality:
the mainstay of love and
the medicine of laughter.

Contents

Introduction

For several years now, people have suggested that the insights about spirituality I have shared in lectures and workshops would be valuable as a book. I articulate what others already know instinctively, and participants request something in print so they can share the affirmation and encouragement they felt with friends and colleagues. A few of my own soulmates have been even more cogent in their repeated urgings and incentives. Among them, Father Carl Last was a primary stimulus in moving me to make such publication a reality. Father Ernest Larkin, O.Carm., and Bishop Kenneth Untener were also effective forces. Most recently, the generosity of Ms. Susan B. Thompson provided the competent assistance

I needed in reworking and refining my ideas into written form.

The result is not a documented work of academic research, but rather the fruit of my own theological reflection upon the meaning of our religious heritage, the cultural moment in which we find ourselves today and the lived experience of religious professionals, committed laity and pastoral ministers of the Catholic church who struggle with the meaning and implication of living daily in the Spirit of Jesus. This, my honest framework, is both the limitation and the richness of my wisdom on the topic.

What I offer here may be called consciousness-raising, a heightening of awareness that comes from putting into words what others already sense to be true and real. When people are assured of not being alone on life's journey, their individual morale and community bonds are strengthened. My sincere hope is that those who read these pages will take heart from the shared experience I dare to name.

In Part One I attempt to explain how our contemporary spirituality is rooted in the religious heritage of the Christian churches. The core focus in Chapter Two on the paschal mystery of Jesus is thoroughly consistent with our ascetical and liturgical tradition. From this perspective Chapter Three articulates the principal characteristics of the spirituality being lived out in the late 1980s by many clergy and laity of the Catholic church in the United States.

Part Two then focuses on a sense of direction in spiritual development for the near future. The horizons of the 21st century challenge us to find ways of coping with an emerging pluralism of spiritualities among the People of God. Finally, in the Epilogue, I hint at my intuition about further evolutions of our spirituality.

Both for today and tomorrow, the degree of resonance between my insights and the life experience of the reader will gauge the truth of those insights.

PART ONE: CONTEMPORARY SPIRITUALITY

Books on spirituality are common and many. They vary one from another in degree of depth and breadth. They also vary in their method of approaching the topic of spirituality. Some focus on the way the author believes good people should think and behave. The way we are supposed to live becomes the goal for aspiration and the hope for inspiration. Such an approach may or may not be helpful for ordinary people struggling with the various members of their household, the routine concerns of their ministry or the mundane issues of their workplace.

In 1972 I was involved with the writing committee commissioned by the U.S. Catholic Bishops that produced the national study entitled *Spiritual Renewal of the American Priesthood*. Even though its examples and applications were particular to American Catholic priests, its basic principles and insights about spirituality were actually common to all Christian people.

The approach to spirituality taken in that study could be called descriptive rather than prescriptive. Rather than tell priests how they should become more spiritual, we simply tried to describe the ways in which real priests were already trying to be spiritual. Probably for that very reason, that paperback volume was exceptionally well received by clergy and laity from coast to coast.

This is what prompts me now to write a

book that is similarly descriptive rather than prescriptive. Instead of telling you how you should live, I would prefer to try to put into words that way you are already living the life of God's own Spirit. I believe there is a power and value in simply naming experience. This then will be my approach here. I do not want to sell a certain brand of spirituality to you. My hope is to heighten your awareness of the spirituality that is already living in you.

To take this approach is to make a presumption about the very meaning of spirituality itself. Therefore let me begin by sharing what I mean when we talk about a person's spirituality.

1

Coping With Life

In my experience, the best and most accurate definition of *spirituality* is simply "how I cope with life." Every individual has a unique way of doing this. It is not as if the holy, churchy types have spirituality and others lack it. Rather, each of us has our own way of coping with life. Everyone, including the atheist, the hedonist and the narcissist, has a spirituality.

A Way of Viewing Life

Spirituality as a way of coping with life always has two components: a way of viewing life and a way of experiencing life.

My way of viewing life is my perspective on the world, the way I consistently interpret reality, my basic attitude about life. For instance, if I held up a glass with water at the half-way mark, some would say the glass is half full and some would say the glass is half empty. Neither is a comment upon the contents of the glass, but rather upon the way we interpret the glass' contents. Optimists and pessimists do not perceive different realities; they perceive the same reality differently. Countless examples from our own lives validate this insight.

Centuries ago the Jewish people were attempting to escape from captivity in Egypt. Through a mysterious convergence of circumstances, accompanied by a providential cooperation of the forces of nature, they made their way to freedom while their captors drowned behind them. A natural scientist could probably give a very plausible explanation of the phenomena that provided the critical opportunity for their escape. But the Judaic interpretation of the Exodus event was a direct intervention of God on their behalf.

When two or more people share a way of viewing life, we speak of a "shared faith vision," a kindred perception or interpretation of life experience. This explanation does not discount the authenticity of faith. The First Vatican Council thought almost one hundred

years ago that faith is an act of trust, not a
perfectly rational conclusion of logic. Faith is a
personalized bias, warranted even if not
necessarily self-evident. "Old-Church"
Catholics may feel that this insight is
problematic. Many of us grew up thinking of
faith as our privileged way of knowing what's
really out there rather than as our shared way
of trusting or interpreting a vision of reality.
Think of the countless examples in the gospels
when Jesus credits the ability of people to
trust in his divinity. There would be no value
or merit involved if they were simply assenting
to self-evident truth.

So, our faith is our way of interpreting
what's out there. Perhaps the best example is
how we Christians interpret physical death as
entrance into eternal life. I am certainly not
disagreeing with this interpretation, since I
believe it with all my heart and soul. But it is
a graced way of seeing the world around us.

A Way of Experiencing Life

The second component in any person's
spirituality is the pattern of behavior that
results from their attitude toward life. I call
this a way of experiencing life. I speak of
behavior and experience because our actions,
not our words, reveal our real beliefs or values.
Over a century ago, Cardinal John Henry
Newman articulated this fact when he made

the distinction between "notional assent" and "real assent." Notional assent refers to those things we think we believe in, and real assent refers to those things we really believe in. For instance, if I claim what I most cherish about autumn is taking a walk in the forest but have not actually done this for fifteen years, one might rightfully suspect this is not a genuine value for me.

When we talk about spirituality, we are talking about our patterns of behavior, our consistent way of experiencing life. I am not a charitable person just because I did something once, by a fluke. Rather, I am a charitable person because I have an established, consistent pattern of behaving charitably.

Our way of viewing life shapes our way of experiencing life and, in turn, our life experiences shape our continuing or changing ways of viewing life. I call these two components of our spirituality attitude and behavior. Our Christian and Roman Catholic ascetical heritage identifies the two components of spirituality as contemplation and action. But the mystics and ascetical writers used these words to refer to the same qualities that today we would call attitude and behavior.

One practical implication of this insight is a clearer understanding of what it means to speak of the spirituality of the Benedictines or the spirituality of the Jesuits or the spirituality of diocesan priests or the spirituality of American Catholics in the late 1980s. To the extent that two or more persons share a way of coping with life, that is, a way of viewing and of experiencing life, we can speak of a shared, communal, or group spirituality.

Two Kinds of Spirituality

There are two fundamentally different kinds of spirituality. We can cope with life from the framework of the ideal or from the framework of the real. In other words, our spirituality can proceed deductively or inductively.

Spirituality of the Ideal

I call the first way of coping with life the spirituality of the ideal. In this spirituality, a person's basic reference is an ideal concept, such as "the ideal Christian," "the ideal priest" or "the ideal parent." Based upon the data of our heritage about such an ideal, we deduce appropriate behaviors (the ideal Catholic does such and such). This kind of spirituality generates a litany of "shoulds" and "supposed to's."

In the spirituality of the ideal, the recurring question is "How am I doing?" that is, "How do I match up to that ideal?" Self-critique or the examination of conscience becomes paramount. Inevitably, this results in a spiritual inferiority complex. No matter how long or how arduously I strive to approximate the ideal, I continually fall short. Since I am human flesh and blood, I never seem to become fully that mental concept of the way I am supposed to be.

The process here is deductive, that is, deducing what I am supposed to be like, in light of the ideal. Introspection, when I am consciously trying to be spiritual, is key. So in times of prayer, annual retreat or meetings with a spiritual director, I check myself out against the ideal. From over 20 years of ministering to priests, I can testify to my ability to trigger instant guilt in any group of priests simply by asking "How's your spiritual life these days?" However they may view their spirituality, one thing is certain: it's not good enough in comparison to what it's supposed to be.

In the spirituality of the ideal, what you are supposed to be is dictated by the inherited rules of the group to which you belong and is somehow contained in the ideal.

Spirituality of the Real

A completely different kind of spirituality I call the spirituality of the real. It differs from the spirituality of the ideal primarily at its starting point. It begins with an acknowledgment of reality rather than an ideal concept. I identify my real life experiences, events and relationships. I also claim responsibility for them as truly mine. I then move to discernment by asking, "What is the movement of the Spirit of God within these real life experiences, events or relationships?"

This approach follows an inductive method rather than deducing appropriate behaviors from principles and truths. In the spirituality of the real, the recurring question is not "How am I doing?" but rather "What is God doing in my life?" The key issue is not self-critique but rather discerning the movement of the mystery of God in the mystery of my real human life. This spirituality is Christ- or God-centered, rather than self-centered.

To pursue the mystery of God contained within human experience demands deep faith and openness to conversion. To live a spirituality of the real demands the maturity of the psychological principle of individuation, as well as the spiritual formation of individual Christian conscience. The faculties of mind, heart and will must be brought to bear in discernment. To keep the process from being self-deceptive, we need to use the sound criteria of discernment wisely taught by our Catholic tradition. These criteria include resonance with scripture and with the larger ecclesial experience. The risk of the spirituality of the real is that instead of certitude we have only a reasonable probability in the discernment of Spirit. Many American Catholics today are discovering their ability to live this spirituality of the real with greater self-confidence. Coping with the real world *is* our spirituality.

Recall that the Old Testament has revealed God as "I Am Who Am." God can be found in anything that *is*. However, I Am Who Am can never be found in *what is not*. For instance, all of our "shoulds" are not, at least not yet! The God who *is* can be found in anything real, even if that reality is human weakness, imperfection, even sin. In our tradition, people have had an encounter with God even in the dregs of their sinfulness. However, I Am Who Am can never be encountered in all those idealistic but non-existent expectations we lay upon ourselves and others. For instance, in some parishes the pastor feels that this would be a great parish if he only had a different (ideal) group of parishioners. Sometimes parishioners feel that this would be a great parish if they only had a different (ideal) pastor. As long as we measure each other's shortcomings by an imaginary "ideal," we do not encounter Christ in our Christian communities. At best, we encounter only faint mirrors of ourselves. We have a better chance to encounter Christ among us when we accept one another as we are.

We need to distinguish whether our spirituality is about coping with life's ideals or about coping with real life.

A Mixed Bag

I do not believe that any one of us actually lives either the spirituality of the ideal or the spirituality of the real totally. Rather, most of us have a shifting blend of both spiritualities. We generally allow one to dominate, but occasionally we lapse into the other as well.

Many religious professionals were formed in the spirituality of the ideal. But we have gradually moved, at least in certain areas, into the spirituality of the real due to our pastoral sensitivity and/or personal process of maturation. Many priests operate out of the spirituality of the real in dealing with their people, especially in the context of counselling or spiritual direction. Yet they revert back to a spirituality of the ideal when dealing with themselves. Such "schizophrenia" is both common and understandable in our changing times. The more educated, self confident and "individuated" in conscience Christians become, the more they seem to move toward the spirituality of the real, at least in some aspects of their spiritual lives, a natural process of development from "child" to "adult" in faith.

This development from one kind of

spirituality to another seems to be closely connected to our degree of interaction with those who differ from us. The tension of attempting to cope with contradictions, opposing forces or the existential pluralism contributes the most to developing a spirituality of the real.

The main point is not to judge one spirituality as right and the other as wrong. Rather, my intent is simply to provide helpful handles for naming the spirituality predominantly operative in each one of us.

2

Coming Alive

The next question we must raise is: "What is it about one's way of coping with life that makes it specifically Christian?" The most common misunderstanding is that Christian spirituality is a way of coping with life in terms of the person of Jesus Christ. While that may be some individuals' piety, it is not the answer provided by 2000 years of religious heritage. According to centuries of liturgical and ascetical tradition, what makes our spirituality Christian is that we cope with life in terms of an activity of Jesus Christ, specifically the death and resurrection of Jesus.

Our heritage as Catholic Christians teaches that the hallmark of Christian spirituality is the dying and rising of Jesus. For instance, all of the sacramental rituals of the church are understood as ways of participating in some aspect of this activity of Christ Jesus. Christian liturgy ritualizes Christian spirituality. This core mystery of our faith is called the "paschal mystery of Jesus." Anyone who has studied the ascetical or liturgical heritage of our church will immediately recognize this phrase that sums up the basics of our Christian faith and spirituality. It is central to what we are all about as Christians, but what is its full significance?

The Paschal Mystery of Jesus

Which Jesus?

The first and perhaps most important word that demands clarification is *Jesus.* We need to focus on this because in our tradition we speak of the Jesus of history and the Jesus of faith. Although essentially related, they are distinct.

We know the Jesus of history was male, Jewish, and foster-child of a carpenter. He lived in the town of Nazareth in the ancient Middle East. Because his teachings and his ways upset the religious institution in which he was devoutly involved, he was executed as a criminal outside the walls of Jerusalem. According to our tradition, after this Jesus of history died, he was raised up by the Father to become the Lord of the new creation, the head of the church. After his resurrection he becomes the Jesus of faith. From St. Paul we know the Jesus of faith is the One "in whom there is no east or west," no Jew or Gentile, no male or female, no slave or free (Gal 3:28; Rom 10:12; Col 3:11; Eph 4:5). We encounter the Jesus of faith where "two or three are gathered in his name" (Mt 18:20). We come to know this Jesus in our faith-filled relationships with each other.

The whole point of St. John's gospel is that the Jesus Christians know by faith is the same Jesus the apostles and first disciples knew in the flesh. Through this Jesus of faith, Christians can enter into relationship with the Father in the Spirit in the same way as those who walked and talked with the Jesus of history. Similarly, St. Paul claimed to be a genuine apostle because of his relationship to the Jesus of faith even though he did not personally know the Jesus of history. The fact of this equality of relationship through the Jesus of history or the Jesus of faith so stressed by John and Paul makes no sense unless they were aware of a distinction between the two.

Many Roman Catholics today, at all levels of the hierarchy and in the church at large, often seem to miss or to ignore this critical distinction. Instead, we hear evidence of "fuzzy thinking." For instance, some claim that to be a Catholic priest one must bear a likeness to Jesus. If that implies a likeness to the Jesus of faith, I, for one, would wholeheartedly agree. But if that implies a likeness to the Jesus of history, then, at least logically, one must not only be a male but must also be of Jewish lineage in order to be a priest. I do not think many Roman Catholic clergy would care to pursue this much further!

A number of signals reveal whether a person's spirituality emphasizes the death and resurrection of the Jesus of history or the Jesus of faith. The preacher whose personal spirituality focuses more upon the Jesus of history leads the congregation to believe that all the really important things happened 2000 years ago. In our lives today, we should do such and such based upon Jesus' past good example. For instance, we should strive to imitate the compassion Jesus showed to sinners. In contrast, the homilist whose personal spirituality focuses more upon the Jesus of faith leads the congregation to recognize that the scriptures are "being fulfilled in our hearing" today. Our attention is called to the marvelous works of God among us in the present moment. For instance, when we accept back into our home and heart a son or daughter who has strayed from the values we taught them, the compassion of Jesus is alive in us.

The clear and dominant emphasis in our

liturgical heritage is upon the Jesus of faith. If you were to look carefully in the Sacramentary, you would see the opening prayers for each Mass, vernacular translations of prayers that have been offered in the church's official liturgical books for approximately 1600 years! You will notice in those prayers, for instance during the season of Lent and Eastertime, that the only reference to the Jesus of history is in the opening clause, for example, "O God, you who did not spare your only Son an ignominious death upon the cross. . . ." But the thrust of the body of the oration is always focused upon the Jesus of faith, for example, ". . . grant that by our Lenten discipline, we may come to Easter glory."

Therefore, when we say that Christian spirituality focuses upon the death and resurrection of Jesus, our tradition teaches that the emphasis is upon the Jesus of faith, the experiences of death and resurrection occurring among those in the community of faith today. The devotional Stations of the Cross ritualize in prayer the death and resurrection of the Jesus of history as food for reflection today. However, the official liturgy of the church, the Mass, ritualizes the death and resurrection of the Jesus of faith. It brings to communal prayer our participation in that mystery today, through the sorrows and joys, the pains and hopes, of our daily lives.

Understanding the full significance of Jesus is perhaps the most challenging part of grasping a Christian spirituality focused upon the paschal mystery of Jesus. Mystery and paschal are easier to understand.

Mystery

In our ordinary use of the word *mystery*, we mean something concealed from our understanding. In our phrase, the paschal mystery of Jesus, *mystery* translates the Greek *misterion* or the Latin *sacramentum*. This more technical use of the word does include the connotation that something is partially revealed and partially concealed. But more importantly it also means that to the extent something is revealed, it is also simultaneously achieved. The phrase "paschal mystery of Jesus" emphasizes the fact that something is being accomplished in the act of its being revealed.

St. Paul uses the word *mystery* in this way when he speaks about the mystery of our salvation in Christ Jesus (see Eph 1:9, Eph 3:5, Col 1:24-29). Sacramental theology also uses mystery in this way, for example proclaiming the mystery of faith in the memorial acclamation of the eucharistic liturgy.

Paschal

The final word we need to clarify is *paschal*, derived from the Judaic concept of passover (*pasch*), the journey of the Hebrew people from slavery in Egypt to the Promised Land. A paschal experience is a passage experience, a transition, a movement from one way of being in the world to another. We might compare this to the concept of seasons or passages in human development cited in contemporary psychology.[1]

Moreover, in our Christian heritage, we speak of the concept of the handing oneself over to some form of death so that new life might emerge. St. Paul, for instance, reminds us of this action of *kenosis* or self-emptying on the part of Jesus in Phil 2:6-11. The implication is that this type of life-transition occurs as the result of an inner choice, not as something that happens to a passive victim, like a handicap from a car accident. We enable the passage or at least freely cooperate in its occurrence, by handing ourselves over to the process. For example, moving from adolescence into adulthood or getting beyond a mid-life crisis are passage experiences that only occur when we are ready to let go. We only learn the wisdom of "no pain, no gain" after we reluctantly agree to this condition for growth and development and deliberately place ourselves in a new frame of reference.

In summary, the paschal mystery of Jesus refers to those social and individual experiences of dying and rising in the community of faith by which we are united, through the power of the Holy Spirit, with

Christ Jesus. Sometimes this is a physical process, as when "we make up in our bodies what is lacking in the sufferings of Christ" (Col 1:24). More often though it is a psychological process of consciously letting go of one way of being in the world so that we can come alive to some new way. By faith, we believe that when we do this, the death and resurrection of Christ Jesus is being enfleshed or incarnated in our human experiences. The process of coming alive is at the heart of Christian spirituality.

With a clearer grasp of the paschal mystery of Jesus as the hallmark of a Christian spirituality, we can turn our attention to the process of spiritual development that follows from this kind of spirituality.

The Process of Christian Spiritual Development

As you might well imagine, the process of Christian spiritual development involves becoming one with the dying and the rising of Jesus Christ, letting the dying of Christ become enfleshed in us and letting the rising of Christ show forth in our lives. I prefer to express this process in more personal language as embracing the sore points of my life and reaching out to others.

Embracing My Sore Points

First, a sore point is the secret that I would be mortified if anyone found out about me, my fatal flaw, my constant weakness, my magnificent obsession. For instance, some priests talk about the terrible first pastor they had or some married people talk about a disagreement they had with their brother or sister-in-law years ago.

Sometimes a sore point is rooted so far back in our personal history that we have no memory of its origins. We may even need professional help to get in touch with the childhood or pre-natal experiences that have left lasting scars upon our psyche. Support groups such as Adult Children Of Alcoholics help people cope with tragic early experiences or deficiencies in personality development that go back to childhood.

Whatever their individual story, many people today bear a cross throughout their lives—a wound from the past that has never been adequately healed, a traumatic experience that has scarred them for life in some way, a personal awareness about some aspect of who they are that continues to trouble them, or a deficiency in attempting to live life to the full.

The common way we deal with sore points

is to deny or express them, to displace them onto others, or to try to escape them. Many in our society cope with the loss of a beloved in death or divorce in this way. The Christian way of coping with sore points is to embrace them, perhaps because the Christian believes that if you embrace the cross of Christ, you get Christ too, at no extra charge. Christians have the courage to embrace the sore points of life because of their faith in the resurrection.

By embracing our sore points, we claim responsibility for them. Sometimes it is helpful to name or identify our sore points verbally to another, for example a counselor, spiritual director or therapist. When we become comfortable with our sore points, we accept all of who we are, weaknesses as well as strengths. In Jungian psychology, this is called making friends with your shadow. We each have not only a bright side but also a shadow side. By making friends with our shadow, we learn to live peacefully with our imperfections as part of our reality.

This process of embracing our sore points is somewhat like learning to live with arthritis. Some people suffer arthritic pain to such an extent that it dominates who they are and the way they live life. They confine themselves to sitting at home feeling their pain and feeling sorry for themselves. Yet, others experience equal pain but determine that it will not define their lives. They put their arthritic pain into a larger perspective and do their best to live a normal life.

These people embrace their sore points. They have learned to accept their imperfections and to make the best of life's limits. They clearly identify their sore point, assume responsibility for integrating it into their life, and attempt to locate themselves in a broader perspective.

Outreach to Others

The spirituality of the paschal mystery of Jesus involves rising as well as dying. A temptation for some is to want to linger in the place of death. This desire may be called martyr spirituality, but it certainly is not Christian spirituality.

If we seek the risen Jesus in our lives, we must look beyond the tomb. We have to learn the same lesson as the holy women disciples of Jesus on that first Easter morn. They went to the tomb to find Jesus. But the angel had to enlighten them: "You are looking for Jesus of Nazareth, who was crucified; he has risen, he is not here . . . He is going before you to Galilee; it is there that you will see him" (Mk 16:6-7).

The experience of the resurrection is not to be found in the tomb. After we have died to some aspect of ourselves, we must look beyond the tomb of self in outreach to others.

Imagine that you are undergoing a profound dying experience. You find yourself in an unlimited void in cold darkness. Your arms move aimlessly in search of something to grab onto. You are distraught, feeling the pain of despair. You feel nothing to give you a sense of security or meaning. This dark night of the soul may last for months, even years. Then one day, in that aimless movement, your fingertips make contact with another set of human fingertips. Stunned, you realize that someone else out there is experiencing what you are experiencing! Everything in you wells up with compassion and you move toward that unknown person to minister at their tomb of death with understanding and care.

We are not aware of the resurrection experience of Jesus while it is happening because it only happens by focusing our attention on someone else's need. Only later do we realize that while we ministered at the tomb of another we moved out of our own tomb. The "coming alive" we have sensed did not occur through intense introspection, waiting and watching for something marvelous to occur. It came when we forgot about ourselves long enough to reach out beyond our own tomb of death.

St. Paul sums it up quite succinctly: "So death is at work in us, but life in you" (2 Cor 4:12). This doesn't mean "Gee, some people have all the luck! I get all the dying and you get all the rising." No! Rather, St. Paul testifies that while he finds the dying experience of Jesus within his own mortal self, he discovers the rising experience in those to whom he ministers.

Ministry is not a corollary to Christian spirituality. Rather, ministry is the core of Christian spirituality. Ministry is the second step of Christian spiritual development. Through outreach to others the rising of Jesus becomes enfleshed in us. Ministry is based on compassion.[2] Because we cope with the dying of Jesus in ourselves, we have the compassion and expertise to stand with our sisters and brothers at their tomb of death. That is how we experience the resurrection of Jesus.

A striking example of this process of spiritual development is a group called Compassionate Friends, a support group of parents who have lost a child through physical death. Often, when a couple loses a child through a tragic death they feel that their family and friends do not truly understand the unique nature of their grief. It is not like suffering the death of a parent, spouse or friend. Eventually, if they are lucky, someone recommends this support group. They discover a forum to share the trauma of their story one more time. But this time, they sense that the listeners understand because the others in this group have themselves lost a child through physical death. They find compassionate, understanding listeners, session after session. Then, one day, another couple joins the group. Now the first parents find themselves in the role of compassionate, understanding listeners. They shift roles from being the recipients of others' ministry to becoming ministers to others.

A pastor I know says this is the nature of every parish community. One week, one half of the parish ministers to the other half. The next week, they switch roles, and the second half now ministers to the first. This is a community of mutual ministry. It is, in effect, how we grow in Christian spiritual development.

Unfortunately, we all can cite countless examples of people who get involved in parish ministry as an escape from embracing their own sore points. But, at least here and there, we do experience people in ministry to others based upon their compassion as fellow pilgrims in the human condition. When we are blessed to know such pastoral ministers, it is truly a wonderful experience. We seem to possess a sixth sense to recognize people in church ministry who are peers to our human condition. This grounds their credibility as spiritual leaders in our lives.

The following image sums up this process of Christian spiritual development. Identify your life's sore points as your cross. How heavy is your cross? How wide is it? How tall is it? Now, bend your cross down and outward toward others. You will find that crosses make excellent bridges! The heavier your cross, the stronger your bridge; the wider your cross, the broader your bridge; and the taller your cross, the deeper your bridge of access into other human hearts. A Christian community is a network of crosses become bridges. A person can die alone, but we only rise in relationship. A vibrant faith community emerges from the process of Christian spiritual development. A group of individuals have chosen to turn the sore points of their lives into avenues of access in relationship with each other.

In the act of turning crosses into bridges we discover the key of a genuinely Christian spirituality: the process of coming alive.

3
Struggling for Vitality

Having explored the meaning of spirituality, especially Christian spirituality, we recognize that spirituality is about life, about the real process of letting go in order to come more fully alive. Christian spirituality is essentially dynamic, not static; it is process spirituality. Our spirituality is no longer striving for a "state of perfection," a static achievement of holiness, but rather an ongoing process of coping with the realities of our daily lives. We allow our experiences of dying to be life-giving, enabling resurrection for others. Our spirituality is our experience of the paschal mystery of the Jesus of faith at work in the world today.

This is true both in our individual lives

and in our life together. The church today is also caught up in the process of spiritual development. We are being asked to let go of the way we *were* as church so that we can come alive to a new way of being church. This paschal conversion of the institutional church is painful. It is accompanied by all the stages of death: denial, blame, bargaining, depression and, for a handful already, acceptance. Whether in our individual lives or in our shared community life, we experience the paschal mystery as a struggle for vitality.

Different authors attuned to the movements of God's Spirit in our day use different vocabulary to name the shadows of sin. Henri Nouwen uses *compulsivity.*[3] Anne Wilson Schaef uses *addiction.*[4] Leonardo Boff uses *pathologies.*[5] Such words recall the recurring images of paralysis or slavery we find throughout scripture. The shadows of sin we detect in our lives, however we name them, consistently oppose the liberated vitality of the children of God coming to fullness in Christ.

Particularly in the second half of the 1980s, certain initiatives on the part of the central administration of the Roman Catholic Church have impressed many as oppressive and demoralizing. The effort to reinstate a pre-Vatican II world of unquestioning obedience to a single perspective seems both reactionary to the liberating spirit that began to emerge 25 years ago and also obsessed with a self-serving agenda in maintaining hierarchical superiority. Because of this reactionary movement, institutional authority has lost credibility and the church at times has been pervaded by a stifling atmosphere of deadening atrophy. The struggle for vitality is taking place in an ecclesiastical system where many feel helpless and hopeless because a few people need power and control.

Much of this battle is being fought by weapons of words that conceal rather than reveal intention. The imaginative vocabulary of a vibrant church is co-opted to disguise an opposite style of church governance. Church leaders adopt the art of nuanced word-crafting to maintain unity at all costs. Equivocation and nominalism become strategies for survival.

The struggle for vitality prompts others to use charged words in an attempt to jar the system to its senses. Matthew Fox, for example, has used phrases such as "a dysfunctional family" and "creeping fascism" in his effort to communicate in a way that might possibly effect insight.[6]

In his open letter to Cardinal Ratzinger in 1988, he noted evidences of such malaise in recent patterns of Catholic church leadership. By contrast, the creation spirituality he advocates, which presumes a fresh approach to educational method (right *and* left brained) and to cosmology, mysticism and art, is grounded in a movement of the Spirit that is healthy, liberating and energizing. Out of love for the well-being of the church, such prophet-like critics prompt diagnosis and remedy of whatever sickness interferes with the church's mission to contemporary society.[7] Their words identify the current malaise as a form of addiction that deadens or atrophies the Body of Christ.

In such a scenario, vitality is needed. Vitality is the proof of the presence and power of God. The Spirit of God breaths new life into the dead bones of a church not yet buried. We see this vitality in the modern-day prophet who will not be silenced, in the small group dynamics of a parish RENEW program, in the Sunday worship of a vibrant parish, in the senior citizen awaking to a potential for lay ministry, in the impetuous generosity of a teen club bringing groceries to shut-ins, or in the efforts of a pastor to persevere in pastoral sensitivity despite what the chancery says. Perhaps one of the greatest signs of the church's vitality is the struggle of competent women for equal opportunities for church ministry. That they continue to struggle, continue to hope, continue to make small inroads here and there gives evidence of paschal mystery spirituality. Church authorities consciously alienate other groups, such as loyal gay/lesbian Catholics. That these groups refuse to disappear gives added hope to

VITAL SPIRITUALITIES

all who continue to struggle for vitality. That so many lay people, priests and even bishops are willing to continue to struggle for their just rights in the church is an ongoing sign of the Spirit among us, the Spirit we call vitality.

While there is undoubtedly a pluralism of spiritualities thriving side by side in the church today, in my pastoral work in Chicago and across the country I have witnessed a shared faith vision from which many committed laity and pastoral ministers live in the Spirit. Occasionally I refer to this brand of spirituality as "contemporary American Catholic spirituality." But that is a misnomer, both because many of God's people who are not Roman Catholics live this spirituality and also because it is definitely not the operative spirituality of many devout Roman Catholics in America today. So, rather than give it a name, let me describe three of its characteristics, each a facet of the struggle for vitality.

Even though I personally identify with this spirituality, I hope my personal investment will not be taken as a judgment that other brands of spirituality are less worthy of contemporary Christianity. I hope my description of a "real" spirituality for some of us will not be interpreted as a prescription of "shoulds" for some new "ideal" spirituality.

The struggle for vitality that characterizes this spirituality many of us now attempt to live has three facets: the struggle for balance, the struggle for liberation and the struggle for mutuality.

Struggling for Balance

Many of us in the church today experience the paschal mystery of Jesus as a struggle for balance in our lives. Some pastoral ministers struggle for balance between professional role and personal identity. Sometimes this is a time management issue. We can neglect family, friends, recreation, prayer and other personal needs because of the press of ministry's demands upon us. But at a deeper level it is an issue of meaning—the meaning we choose to create for ourselves. I can become so engrossed in my ecclesial role that I am no longer in touch with any personal identity apart from that role. Retirement or any transition within the routines of that role becomes traumatic because I no longer know who I am apart from the role. Many church ministers today struggle to provide nourishment and development for these real and complementary sides of their life.

Other pastoral ministers struggle to balance the required with the desired responsibilities of their ministry. For instance, many pastors feel torn between the responsibilities of parish administrator and the responsibilities of spiritual leader. Some express this frustration as "not having functioned as a priest since the day they became pastor." Such a statement expresses a lack of balance in their use of time as well as a value judgment about their administrative responsibilities.

Many Catholics today express this struggle for balance as the attempt to integrate disparate parts of their experience: youthful idealism with practical realism in daily living, personal convictions with public policies taught by the church, inherited faith values with new horizons of experience.

The struggle for balance is, at root, a struggle for personal wholeness, that deep sense of integrating the various parts of our real selves. When we finally reach this inner wholeness, we are balanced despite the forces pulling us in so many directions.

We see this same struggle for integration in the worldwide community. A growing number of Catholics no longer espouse the old dualism which was Hellenistic philosophy's contribution to church tradition. They struggle to integrate the sacred and the secular rather than continue to separate reality into categories like church and world, clergy and laity or religion and culture. The Roman Catholic Church today is struggling with the end of what Karl Rahner has tagged the "second epoch of Christianity," or the Eurocentric church.[8] The universal church is no longer held together by the glue of one particular cultural expression. The European model of church can no longer be canonized as "our faith."

Catholics in the United States struggle with the end of the immigrant church for many, while still attempting to respond to new immigrants and the growing Hispanic tenor of American Catholicism. We also struggle with the proper relationship of church and state.

Richard McBrien and Mario Cuomo remind us that the categories of understanding formulated by John Courtney Murray are quickly becoming outdated by our current experience of Catholicism in America.[9] Throughout the 1970s and 1980s, pronouncements by both the U.S. Supreme Court and the U.S. Catholic Bishops fostered this development.

John Courtney Murray's legacy is that doctrinal principles grow out of both political and religious experience. In the attempt to apply those principles to current issues, however, the relationship between religion and politics becomes more clear, more intricate and more consolidated. The 1984 presidential campaign was particularly significant in crystalizing the complexities of controversial issues such as the role of religion in public life. As in any genuine dialogue, both perspectives are influenced by the interaction, and their distinct positions become more fine-tuned.

The dynamics of how each side's methods of argumentation become more and more intertwined is perhaps best captured in the ongoing national debate about abortion. In a society marked by pluralism of thought, a consensus-seeking dialogue promotes mutual understanding and eventually a greater balance and integration of values.

At international, national, local and individual levels a similar struggle to balance and integrate past with future continues to be a dominant characteristic of our spirituality. For us, holiness is not only achieving the balance, but also the paschal process of struggling for that balance. We experience the call to let go of the dualisms that dominated our thought and action, to die to putting reality into artificial compartments. We experience the call to come alive to a new integration, to come alive to new horizons of faith in the 21st century, and to come alive to a new heaven and a new earth in proclaiming the kingdom of Jesus in a unified, global village.

Struggling for Liberation

A second characteristic of the paschal mystery of Jesus is in the struggle for liberation. By liberation, I mean the spiritual "freedom of the children of God" to which St. Paul refers (Rom 8:15-16; Gal 5:1). This is freedom from the slavery of compulsive or addictive behavior that paralyzes so many people in our contemporary society and in our church. The lack of freedom particularly afflicts good-hearted and generous people who have learned to live according to the expectations of others. They live in reaction to their perception or projection of the expectations of others. We commonly find this compulsive addiction among church ministers who seem unwilling, almost unable, to say no to any pastoral need that surfaces around them. They are enslaved to the need to be needed. Such pastoral ministers have unwittingly defined their own sense of importance and self-worth not within themselves but in their value for others. They have yet to experience the psychological process of self-individuation.

The proof of the unhealthiness and unholiness in this phenomenon is its connection with a fatalistic defeatism that makes a mystique of being a victim, sometimes called martyr spirituality. A person acts as victim of a situation, a system or the needs of others, feeling destined to find value only in meeting the needs and expectations of others, and also abdicating any responsibility for this predicament. At issue here is a "death-wish" in which the altruistic behavior of ministry becomes a self-destructive addiction. These people do not genuinely believe in their own self-worth, so they need to prove themselves according to their perception of what others expect. Over time, a seething anger at and resentment of life itself, buried deep within, begins to surface in subtle, if not surprising, ways.

Many courageous believers are beginning to name this malaise within themselves, to recognize the compulsive slavery of their lives and ministries. They are willing to admit that the deep, inner recesses of their souls yearn to move beyond addictive self-destruction. Their hearts are now longing for the fresh air of spiritual freedom that comes to those who assume responsibility for their lives. This movement from slavery to responsible stewardship is a struggle to reject definition by others, to reject subtle desperation as hope, to wiggle loose from a bondage of many years. But at the same time this is a struggle for vitality, a struggle to be born into a new way of life, a struggle for liberation.

Those who are willing to engage in this struggle for liberation live the paschal mystery of Jesus. For us, holiness is not only achieving liberation through the responsible ownership of one's story. Holiness is also the paschal process, the dynamic movement, the struggle for that liberation. We experience the call to let go of our self-pity, to die to the false ego that tries to prove itself to everyone else and to let go of the pseudo-security of our addictive slavery. We experience the call to come alive to self-acceptance, to come alive to the potential of a yes for one who has learned to say no, and to come alive as a prophetic witness of spiritual freedom in an addictive society and a compulsive church.

Struggling for Mutuality

A third characteristic of life in the Spirit today is the struggle for mutuality, a struggle encountered both in church ministry and in our American social systems.

Many in the Roman Catholic Church learned well a "parent-child" model of formation, care and service. We were trained to aspire after idealistic role models whose human weaknesses were rarely noted. If you wanted to be as good as humanly possible, especially if you were an overachiever in pleasing others, the vocation to become a priest, a nun or a missionary was especially attractive. Once having achieved this sublime status, you could consider yourself "exempt" from most of the laws of human life. Then, except with your own kind, you would never have to relate as peer to others again. Care and service understandably took the shape of "Father Pastor" and "Mother Superior." Father and his handful of helpers, rather like Santa's elves, did ministry for everyone else. At best ordinary lay people were relegated to ministry in the marketplace. Ministry was a one-way street.

VITAL SPIRITUALITIES

A gradual movement in church circles has envisioned ministry more as a mutual exchange of God's grace in the act of ministry, an understanding based upon the Second Vatican Council's concept of collegiality. This style of shared responsibility for the church's mission was first seen in the bishops' rapport with each other. Later it became a desirable way of life among all God's people. The sacrament of baptism was rediscovered as the common springboard for all mission and ministry, which eventually evolved into recent insights about collaborative ministry. A diversity of gifts complement each other in the corporate enterprise of the church's mission. A reciprocity of grace is at work, so that you minister to me as I minister to you, preventing the misconception that one person always gives and the other always receives. Genuine ministry is a two-way street.

In mutual or peer ministry, influence, care and service are genuinely reciprocal. We often see such mutuality between husband and wife, or between friends or colleagues. It is based upon the ability to relate to each other out of mutual respect. While we have different roles, we experience basic human equality. One person's opinions, role or spirituality are not cast as superior to the other's. Whether our life experiences are similar or different, we are all fellow pilgrims on a journey through life. This companionship in faith or partnership in ministry presumes a positive regard for one another's competency, equal rights in communication and access to information and an equal relationship as sisters and brothers in the kingdom of Jesus. Ministry based upon mutuality is more mature, and perhaps more authentic, than a parent-child model of ministry.

It is no secret that this sense of mutuality or partnership is still more dream than reality for many in church ministry today. But the struggle to achieve it is very real.

We notice issues of mutuality in how men and women work together in parishes and dioceses, in clergy-lay relationships, in tensions between professionals and volunteers, in justice concerns for church personnel and in the need for equal access to ecclesial leadership positions. How authority is exercised at various levels of church governance probably defines the greatest struggle for collaborative ministry today. But these struggles for a better spirit of partnership in church ministry are just the tip of the iceberg.

The struggle for mutuality is rooted in basic attitudes and behaviors about human relationships in social systems espoused by a culture. In her book, *The Chalice & the Blade*,[10] Riane Eisler explores the historical struggle between partner and dominator models in society. The fundamental paradigms of relationships, rooted deep within our social

unconscious and individual psyches determine
our daily experience of conflict or harmony.
The degree of our inner security, our
integration of the opposing forces within, our
psycho-sexual maturation, our positive
acceptance of ourselves as human and limited,
our capacity for intimacy and our ability to
relate out of shared vulnerability rather than
out of pretended strengths shape our capacity
for mutuality. We must be willing to
collaborate in stewardship of the earth's
resources, and to develop our sense of oneness
with both creation and Creator. The struggle
for mutuality must confront an adversarial
cultural context of competitiveness,
possessiveness, fear, greed and private
enterprise for security and self-
aggrandizement.

It's no wonder that in both our ecclesial
and social systems genuine mutuality is so
difficult to realize. The partnership model may
be a clear goal, at least for some, but it entails
a complex struggle.

The good news though is that holiness
does not lie only in the achievement of
mutuality. Holiness also lies in the struggle
itself. This is true at all levels: interpersonal,
parish, ecumenical, national and
international. We experience the call to let go
of the need to prove our independence, to die
to the roots of our feelings of inferiority and
insecurity, and to let go of that adolescent self-

defense that prompts competitiveness. We experience the call to come alive to our potential to be vulnerable with each other, to being an occasional recipient rather than constant benefactor in the dynamics of mutual service, and to value the honesty of togetherness more than the pretence of independence.

I have described the shape Christian spirituality takes in many lives today. Our experience of the paschal mystery of Jesus is experienced in a struggle for vitality that involves a struggle for balance, liberation and mutuality. I hope that to the extent that my description has resonated with your experience, you will be affirmed. Where we differ, I hope you will reflect upon your experience of the paschal process that is the hallmark of Christian spirituality.

Part Two: Tomorrow's Spiritualities

Having probed some principal aspects of Christian spirituality today, I would like to explore a sense of direction in spiritual development for the 1990s.

I admit that many faithful members of the People of God among us live a different spirituality from the threefold struggle for vitality I described. Some consciously and conscientiously prefer a spirituality of the ideal. Others actually experience the paschal mystery of Jesus by struggling *against* the change inherent in the three-fold struggle. Fidelity to their convictions opposes the development of Catholic doctrine in the direction of what they would consider humanistic secularism. These Catholics are letting go of passive tolerance and coming alive to a militant restoration of the pre-Vatican II church.

Such realities lead us to consider these questions: Why is such a pluralism of spiritualities developing in our communities of faith? How can we cope with this emerging pluralism?

4

Understanding the Pluralism

I have already explained part of the reason why people operate out of different spiritualities. Spirituality depends upon a way of viewing and experiencing life. Some people deduce a moral code from ideals, while others discern the presence and power of God inductively from experience. Some people cope with life dominantly though not exclusively through the historical person of Jesus. Others base their spirituality on the paschal mystery, the dynamic activity of Jesus Christ among us.

Whatever else one's spirituality includes, at least it involves a way of viewing and experiencing God, self, others and the world. The variables in these four facets of reality explain the pluralism of spiritualities we find in our society and church today.

Different Ways of Viewing God

First, people have different and often contrasting ways of viewing God. Some people think God is the direct cause of all the good and evil that happens in the world. God is the immutable Creator and Judge, the ultimate controller and manager of law and order. Our agenda then is to find out what God wants of us in this life and to obey or suffer the consequences. Others, however, see God as the indirect cause of life's good and evil. God invites us to collaborate in the ever-changing divine plan and stands ready to surprise us with ever new horizons and agenda until God steals the last act with a happy ending. We are challenged to respond to the God of this unfolding and, at times, unravelling scenario with both awe and input.

Whatever a person's God-view, it is interesting to notice any subtle innuendoes about control. Who is controlling whom? Often, ironically, the more someone assigns the quality of "all-controlling" to his or her image of God, the more that person may be subtly trying to control God! To pray to the God who magically controls the outcome of a ball game so that my team will win is, in effect, a way in which I am controlling God. These people become irate or stop believing in God when their prayers are not answered. The attitude seems to be that an all-powerful God is there to answer my prayers. God is my puppet, preventing my pain and providing for my needs. I once commented that religion is thinking we control God while faith is coming to recognize that God controls us.

In many instances, the key issue involved is ultimately a person's image of God. Certain Catholics, for example, used to find security and comfort in their pre-Vatican II experience of church. Vatican II developments in their parishes disenchanted them. Some have migrated to evangelical, fundamentalist churches. Onlookers wonder how such "traditional" Catholics could change their institutional affiliation. The explanation is quite simple: Their way of viewing God has remained the same over the past 25 years. They have relocated to those settings that offer the same God-view—in effect a modern-day substitute for the pre-Vatican II Catholic church. I am not judging this as good or bad. I am however saying that understanding such people is a matter of spirituality and, more particularly, the way they view and experience God.

Another example of this can be seen in those who find diverse approaches to fund-raising, tithing or sacrificial giving either spiritually appealing or spiritually offensive.

Different approaches presume different ways of viewing God. The motivations underlying church contributions range from attitudes about "God and me" to attitudes about "shared responsibility for my sisters and brothers who reveal God to me." Fund-raising strategies that presume contributors' fear or guilt in facing a just Judge, or the need to guarantee eternal salvation by a sound investment portfolio can sometimes more effectively generate revenue than appeals that presume shared responsibility by stewardship of our resources.

In any case, there are not merely two or twenty, but unlimited ways of viewing God. My point is that this great variety is a principal factor in explaining the diversity of spiritualities we find around us today.

Different Ways of Viewing Self

Second, people have different and often contrasting ways of viewing themselves. Some people have a negative self-image. They feel they have little intrinsic value, and sometimes find their only redeeming worth in helping or pleasing others. Such people often engage in unconscious and self-destructive patterns of addictive or compulsive behavior. Consider, for instance, the housewife who forever prepares meals for neighbors she feels sorry for, or the pastor who tries but cannot answer every ring of the phone or doorbell. Such people then wallow in self-pity, moaning about not having time for themselves. They disregard their own needs (presumably because they don't feel their needs are important) and then unwittingly blame others for the neglect they feel! *That* is self-destructive behavior.

Others have a healthy and positive self-image, appreciating their intrinsic worth as uniquely gifted by God. Such people live with a comfortable awareness of their limits and limitations. They serve others out of inner freedom and generally approach situations with self-confidence, self-acceptance and flexibility. Consider for instance the housewife who gifts herself with a half-hour of quiet time at the beginning of each day or the pastor who enlists someone to answer the phone and door so that he can have an hour to unwind in the late afternoon. They provide for their own legitimate needs for some privacy out of a sense of their own importance and worth and then care for others more cheerfully because they don't use this service to make themselves feel important.

The unlimited variety of ways of viewing oneself helps explain the diversity of spiritualities we find around us today. I think a good part of the reason people view themselves differently has to do with how they cope with their own basic needs. Every human person has three fundamental psychological needs: the need to feel important, the need to feel secure and the need to feel loved. For instance, the examples above address the ways some people cope with the need to feel important, to feel that one's life has value or significance. The other two basic psychological needs, security and belonging, judging by my pastoral experience of how people cope with them, also give tremendous insight into a person's spirituality. These needs motivate us.

How we cope with our needs often becomes most visible in the way we interact with others. For example, we all need to feel secure. But how do we meet that need? I may try to control those around me, hoping they won't change so I can feel secure in thinking everything around me is stable. Or I may have dealt with my sources of anxiety consciously and deliberately, gradually learning to feel comfortable with changes in the world around me. In meeting the need to belong, I may attach myself to every passing face or fad in desperate escape from being alone. Or I may meet my belonging needs by taking the time and patience to nurture friendships, cherishing them as valuable in my life.

Healthy people deal with these three human needs consciously, deliberately and up-front. Unfortunately, all too many seem to deal with these needs unconsciously, unwittingly and obliquely. The degree of consciousness about the way one copes with these motivating needs makes the most significant difference in the way people view themselves.

We all interpret experiences. We each have our own attitude about and way of experiencing any situation. Yet some people do not recognize that they are interpreting. They believe that "the way I see it is the way it is." Recognizing that I am interpreting involves at least some degree of conscious awareness of my motivation. "I viewed the comment as an attack because I usually internalize feedback in a negative way." To know why I interpret an experience, situation or relationship the way I do is the beginning of real wisdom and the ground of understanding my unique spirituality. Unless I can recognize and respect the distinctiveness of my subjective attitudes, I cannot accept or respect the common ground underlying a pluralism of spiritualities.

When we are unaware of why we do what we do, our view of self is deceptive at best and often downright false. The greater objective self-knowledge we possess, the more we can be true to ourselves and true to the Giver of life.

Different Ways of Viewing Others

The third factor in understanding different spiritualities has to do with how a person views others. For example, some people view others as competitors. I need to prove myself to those around me. Others become the enemy, even in spirituality. In the classic work *The Imitation of Christ* Thomas a Kempis says he feels less holy, less close to God, after he has been out among others. Other people view others not as competitors but as companions on a journey. In my relationship with God, others are not obstacles but rather windows. Through the experience of shared vulnerability my God becomes our God and the ultimate mystery of faith is experienced.

In addition to a plurality of ways of viewing others, shifts also occur within these viewpoints. Perhaps one of the most significant contemporary developments in our communities of faith has been a radical shift toward including others in our spirituality. This sometimes gradual change in attitudes is an indication of the Spirit of God breathing new life among us. Many Roman Catholics were raised to think of sacraments as private matters between God and me: *my* salvation, *my* sanctification. Turning the altar around so that the presider became part of a community of worshipers, exchanging the sign of peace and receiving holy communion from lay ministers of the Eucharist have prompted significant shifts in spirituality because people's way of viewing others radically changed. For many, liturgies are now more clearly communal celebrations of God with us.

When we speak of "the church . . . we" rather than of "the church . . . they," or when we come to identify more fully with a sense of our God rather than just my God, a significant development of attitude occurs. It not only implies a shift in how I view myself, but also a shift in how I view others. This happens regularly in the small group faith sharing; in support groups for those willing to admit an addiction, hurt or weakness; and among the growing number of laity involved in the ministry of care to the sick, homebound or bereaved. Differing attitudes about one another in our communities of faith establish an emerging pluralism of spiritualities.

Different Ways of Viewing the World

How a person views the world is the fourth factor in understanding the pluralism of spiritualities. Spirituality always includes a way of relating to a total life-context. A way of viewing one's environment is the framework for one's way of being in this world.

A person's world can range from the immediate setting to the planet and universe in which we live. It can range from the people with whom we live and work each day to our American or international society. Within the church, one's world can be a local parish or the global community of the People of God. My environment can be viewed in ecological, social, political, economic, religious, cultural, philosophical or psychological terms. The scope of my attitudes and behaviors will influence the breadth or depth of my world. What constitutes my world and how I feel about it are critical factors in shaping my spirituality.

For instance, many of us today are becoming better attuned to the role our physical bodies, the ecological balance of planet Earth and larger galactic forces play in a wholistic and incarnational spirituality. A sense of co-responsibility and stewardship for limited resources is vital to those who are consciously connected with their environment. A sense of identification with nature and its symbolisms in a creation-centered spirituality is in contrast to a dualistic view of matter and spirit in an over-emphasis on the doctrine of redemption.

We recognize that everyone's world-view contains a whole array of conscious and unconscious premises: theological, anthropological, historical, ethical, scientific and symbolic assumptions. Once we grasp all that is connoted by a person's world-view, we clearly see why different ways of viewing the world effects a pluralism of spiritualities. Physicists, whose understanding of the principles of relativity and of quantum mechanics in outer space is an essential part of their spirituality, will ordinarily find little in common with those whose spiritual life in a retirement home focuses on a private devotion to the Infant of Prague. The church's attempts to provide spiritual leadership needs to recognize such diversity of world-views. Its members no longer share a single world of reference, whether spiritual or otherwise!

In understanding one's world-view, one's grasp of the relationship of nature and grace, as well as of culture and religion, will be key. Some world-views will be clearly dualistic and others will be clearly wholistic. In my opinion, as we move into the 21st century, the ability to integrate the secular and the sacred will be perhaps the paramount issue in a mature Christian's world-view. The ability to express that integration in imaginative or symbolic, rather than literal, language will be equally critical. As long as a diversity of world-views continues, a pluralism of spiritualities will necessarily follow.

Even today, we find that people locate the identity and mission of the church in the context of different world-views. Some see only the world of the church! As though they were looking into the open side of a doll house, they see neatly organized rooms in which ecclesiastical roles function. The hierarchical divisions from floor to floor are clear-cut. An astute observer may even notice that the little staircases don't really go through from one floor to the next. Only minimal attention is given to the front-side or to the image projected to outsiders. Ministry refers to what happens within the world of the doll house church. Pastors and pastoral ministers who allow their parish and its daily routines to define their interests and involvements readily understand the games that can be played with a doll house.

Others see the global village as the context for the church. The existential framework for life shifted for these people after they saw that photograph of the "big, blue-green marble" snapped by astronauts returning from the moon. From that moment, the human race was confronted with a new world-view. Christians with this perspective usually possess a sense of the church's mission to proclaim the kingdom of God in a similar framework. This vision of ministry can be found in the Second Vatican Council's document *Gaudium et Spes* ("The Church in the Modern World"). Here, the scope of evangelization is not so much to get people to come back to church as it is to collaborate with all who in their own way seek after God with a sincere heart in the promotion of worldwide justice and peace. To join together with other communities of faith in shaping a corporate conscience of spiritual meaning and divinely human values becomes a heartfelt endeavor. Pastors and pastoral ministers who subscribe to this world-view enable the ministry of the baptized around real life issues. They foster parish bonds not as a haven of refuge from the world but as the necessary mutual support needed for outreach to the world.

Growth from the world-view of the doll house to the world-view of the global village is crucial in the development of spirituality today. Because of recent breakthroughs in technology and communications, no individual's world-view can remain stable over any length of time. This fact has profound repercussions upon a catholic, or universal, community of faith.

The universal Roman Catholic Church has been shaken to its roots in recent decades primarily due to such rapid shifts in the world-view of its members. It is naive to think that issues such as the shortage of vocations to the celibate priesthood or vowed religious life, the breakdown of uniform adherence to a tight code of moral conduct, or a growing self-sufficiency of local communities in a semi-congregational model of church order are anything less than necessary consequences of the radical shifts in the world-views of the practicing faithful.

It should be obvious that ways of viewing God, self, others and the world are not four separate factors in a spirituality but rather four windows into one reality. Like the facets of a single diamond, these are dimensions of a single spirituality. Attitudes about God, self, others and the world are internally connected.

Change or development in any one will trigger change in the other three. Experiencing another's love for me will help me become more self-accepting, and often makes me feel closer to God. On the other hand, pain within my body, or in relationship to another makes God seem more distant. Finally, when my way of viewing my world radically changes or expands, where and how I detect the presence and power of God adjusts accordingly. We call the end result of these shifts or conversions spiritual growth or development.

These four facets, with all their variables and interconnections, of every person's experience of reality in my opinion help explain why there are, and have to be, a pluralism of spiritualities in our society and church today.

5

Becoming Comfortable With Pluralism

How do we cope with the inevitable pluralism of spiritualities? It seems quite impossible to attempt to dictate the way the People of God should view and experience God, self, others and the world. Neither would I suggest denying or fighting the pluralism.

Learning to cope with pluralism offers us a crucible for spiritual maturation. As we move into the 21st century of our ecclesial history, this will be a major issue of spiritual development in our individual lives and in the pastoral life of the church.

One learns to cope with pluralism primarily by accepting it and learning to be comfortable with it! Obviously, this is easier said than done. Just as many of us struggle for vitality, we will also struggle to become comfortable with pluralism. This struggle has four key components: becoming comfortable with self, with our ecclesial history, with the circus of the Peoples of God and with the paradoxes and incongruities of human life.

Becoming Comfortable With Self

Coming to know yourself objectively is a challenging enterprise. The most difficult part of self-knowledge is what it implies about self-acceptance. Learning to become comfortable with the mixed blessing of who I really am is a life-long endeavor.

Such honesty with self, however, is fundamental to spiritual growth and a foundation for coping with the pluralism of spiritualities. I cannot accept others as they truly are, as different from myself, until I have accepted my own blend of strengths and weaknesses. Objective self-knowledge and wholehearted self-acceptance give a person the inner security that enables non-defensive acceptance of diversity in and among others.

Learning to be comfortable with yourself demands that you let go of masks that hide your true self. This process of individuation, of owning my true identity in faith, includes a sense of losing the faith I inherited. This is the precise intent of the gospel imperatives: "Unless a grain of wheat fall to the ground and die, it remains but a single grain . . . " (cf. Jn 12:24) and "If you want to be my follower, renounce yourself, take up your cross every day and follow me; for those who want to save their lives will lose them, but those who lose their lives for my sake will save them" (cf. Lk 9:23-25). As faithful followers of Jesus, we do not fear this loss because we have already come to know, from personal experience, that in Christ all loss becomes gain.

Whatever words we use to express this mystery of our faith, the basic truth is "What's real is real!" I am challenged to put aside my masks and make-up, so I can see myself as I really am, with all of my strengths and weaknesses. I put aside a solely intellectual faith and take up the faith I really live. I am challenged to accept my true face!

The false self in each of us tends to idealize others, just as it has idealized itself as who we really are. We are tempted to pretend that someone else is the ideal or privileged other, the perfect manifestation of my fantasy of self. Such a grandiose vision can be accompanied by depression from sensing the deception involved.[11] When we mature, we allow others to be truly "other" and to be less than ideal. Letting go involves accepting reality as the new norm. Accepting what is real in me enables me to accept unconditionally what is in other people and the world.

I accept the fact that my true face, with all

its blemishes, is acceptable. Once I no longer need the pretense of my false self, I can accept the limits of who others truly are. I no longer demand that they wear idealized masks. When I do so, I accept the framework of reality by accepting the limits of others.

Becoming comfortable with myself unmasked is thus the first step in genuinely accepting others, the first component of learning to cope with the pluralism of spiritualities.

Becoming Comfortable With Our Ecclesial History

Becoming comfortable with the pluralism of spiritualities challenges us to become comfortable with the facts of our history as the People of God. Just as we need to break through the facade of the idealized self, we need to break through our idealized concept of the church to become comfortable with the real facts and limitations of our ecclesial identity.

Bishop Ken Untener of Saginaw, Michigan, has a favorite drawing of hundreds of little fish, each one representing two thousand years of history. To begin to count the number of fish becomes mind-boggling. The last fish in the lower right-hand corner is a different color than the rest; this last one coincides with the brief life of the church in the panorama of the millions of years of planet Earth's history. Such a perspective, he observes, radically changes our understanding of the phrase "as we have *always* taught!" In relationship to the cosmos of galaxies and even life on this planet, the story of the Catholic church is still in the first stage of development.

If we focus on this most recent 2000 years, looking carefully at the facts of church history, we further discover the phenomenon of discontinuity as a characteristic of ecclesial development. In the history of the New Testament we find: 1) the experience of God revealed in the events of human history, 2) a tradition shaped by handing down remembered experience from generation to generation, until 3) a discontinuity of experience, for example, the destruction of the temple in Jerusalem, reshapes the tradition, while 4) continuing to reveal the mystery of God still at work in the new events of human history.

These moments of discontinuity are sometimes described as quantum leaps, a term that refers more to a sudden movement of tremendous energy than to bridging an extensive distance. A quantum leap may be a movement of very slight distance. Tremendous energy builds up until the power breaks through and crosses a gap to some new phase of development. A good example is the now famous phrase from the first moon landing:

"One small step for man; one giant leap for mankind." The astronaut's foot moved only a few inches, but as the culmination of years of dreaming, planning and perfecting the journey into outer space, that slight motion jettisoned the human race into a whole new era.

A quantum leap implies an abrupt transition. In instances such as the moon landing, the abruptness is in terms of new horizons of the human imagination, a radical shift in our perception of the earth's relationship to the moon. Historically, a quantum leap may be just a recurrence of an escalating pattern, but it unexpectedly and abruptly refocuses our imaginative framework with a whole new mindset. This kind of discontinuity is more symbolic than factual or literal.

Quantum leaps of symbolic discontinuity are common in our church history. Significant changes occurred after a gradual build-up of energy that could no longer be contained by the status quo. Examples include the Council of Jerusalem in A.D. 70 accepting Gentiles as fellow Christians, the establishment of Christianity as the official religion of the Roman Empire and the Second Vatican Council opening the door to more active lay participation in the life of the church.

Though each of these innovations resulted from a gradual process of historical development, it was experienced as a rather dramatic break from a previous mindset or practice. For instance, the quantum leap of the Second Vatican Council resulted from decades of renewal movements in biblical, liturgical and ecumenical thought, the gradual shift in the college of bishops from predominantly European to international membership and forceful shifts in modern society and its relationship to the church.

Today, as we enter the final decade of this century, the awareness of the incongruity of dualistic attitudes and systems in church life is growing toward another quantum leap of discontinuity.

In the face of the significant transitions taking place in the life of the church as we approach the 21st century, it is especially helpful to recognize the discontinuity and the diversity of tradition in our ecclesial heritage. Once we become comfortable with constant change throughout the history of our church, we become less apprehensive about changes on our immediate horizon. We trust that the mystery of God is still at work in our day.

Some people fear that married and/or women priests, significant strides in ecumenism, lay-led liturgies, priestless parishes, democratic church governance and other changes in church discipline will signal the end of the church. Others fear that the forceful return of pre-Vatican II attitudes and practices, a new breed of conservative and clerical leadership, the suppression of intellectual development and respectful expression of differing opinion (dissent), will mean sudden death for the church. Most likely, we will simply continue to stumble along on our way to the Kingdom. We will bump into each other out of panic and fear, and turn corners we never anticipated. These "end of the world" developments will be mysteriously integrated en route. Then, one day, by an uncanny turn, we will find ourselves beyond the gap in a new space where past and future overlap.

Becoming comfortable with our history as the People of God leads almost automatically to becoming comfortable with a pluralism of spiritualities. Diverse spiritualities are as inevitably a part of our future as they have always been a part of our past. Only those who live in ivory towers, divorced from reality and ignorant of history, can presume it should be otherwise. Consistency and unanimity in pastoral practice and ecclesial spirituality are fantasies for tomorrow by those who imagine what happened yesterday. The more we become comfortable with the limitations and facts of our history, the more we will be comfortable with pluralism in the church.

Becoming Comfortable With the Peoples of God Circus

The struggle to become comfortable with a pluralism of spiritualities involves becoming comfortable with our humanity as the People of God. The phrase I have coined to express this perspective is "becoming comfortable with the peoples of God circus."

Although I wholeheartedly subscribe to the Vatican II vision of the church as the People of God, it probably is more accurate to refer to the "peoples" of God. Both within the Roman Catholic communion and beyond to other faiths, many smaller groupings make up the People of God. The plural form highlights the legitimate differences among all who consider themselves part of the People of God.

The circus is a good image of who we really are—a motley conglomerate of colors, movements, sounds and smells. Many a bustling modern day parish is often and aptly described as a three-ring or ten-ring circus. More is happening than anyone can control. Things often get done haphazardly. One thing is planned and another happens. The incongruities of the human condition sway from the comic to the tragic. The life of the circus cannot be put into neat compartments. It is a life of complexity and paradox, humor and weakness, glitter and pathos. The human condition is imperfect. To be human is to accept people as they really are, not as we would like them to be. Not too long ago, I read an open letter from a teenager to the adults of his parish. He asked that the youth be taken seriously in dialogue and communication, and that the "established" members of his community take the initiative in reaching out to them. The letter concluded with the profound insight that there is "no religion without relationship."

The willingness to enter into and remain in relationship with others ultimately makes formal religion possible. Any society's organizations and systems can survive only as long as individuals are willing to have a functional relationship with other individuals, regardless of whether or not they feel the affective bonds of community. Minimally, we agree to disagree without being disagreeable. Even the toxic relationships people claim to despise are energized by a mysterious, partially unconscious, choice to remain in relationship.

Religious affiliation represents a willingness to be bound together, to be identified with and to be limited by human, imperfect others. Paradoxically, we most often notice others because of their shortcomings. The unity we experience with them is never clean, precise, ideal or romantic. Rather, it is the unity that binds together a three-ring circus, in which the clown we open our arms to is probably looking the other way!

We learn to become comfortable with the pluralism of spiritualities by accepting the reality of limits in all human relationships. When we no longer demand or expect perfection from the other people in our life, when we are genuinely comfortable with the messiness of the human condition, when we acknowledge that the only faith community we have is a far cry from being of "one mind, one heart and one spirit," when we accept the fact that the great People of God is made up of a motley bunch of peoples, when we finally feel at home in the circus of daily life, then a pluralism of spiritualities is no longer a challenge for us. It is simply the way we are.

The gospel tells us that when we are comfortable with the reality of our human relationships we love one another as Christ has loved us (cf. Jn 13:34-35). This "new commandment" is not easily assimilated into behavior. Most of us live with each other in true Christian love only after long struggle and genuine conversion. Wholehearted acceptance of a pluralism of spiritualities means we have learned the love for one another that tells others we are disciples of Christ Jesus. Ultimately, however, a circus is not something one merely learns to accept. A circus is to be enjoyed! We love one another as Christ has loved us when we can finally enjoy each other in our differences, in our shortcomings, in the motley of our disjointed movements and disparate colors, sounds and smells.

Becoming Comfortable With Life's Paradoxes and Incongruities

Through painful struggle one learns to become comfortable with a pluralism of spiritualities by learning to become comfortable with the paradoxes and incongruities at the heart of the mystery of life itself.

The mature person has broken through facades and appearances and no longer fears the truths of life. He or she has discovered that "the truth shall make you free" (Jn 8:32). The novel *The Name of the Rose,* by Umberto Eco vividly depicts the maze of imprisonment created by fear of the truth.

As we grow and develop, we learn that things are not always what they appeared to be. Often they do not turn out the way we had hoped. As a matter of fact, moving beyond the surface appearance sometimes leads to our worst fears being realized. Then we discover the amazing paradox that what we had feared is not the end of the world and actually may be more desirable in the long run than our original scenario.

Novices on life's journey often live with myths such as the expectation that life is "fair"—equally fair for all or at least fair for the good folk. Yet the more we seek a broader and deeper wisdom when such myths evaporate, the more supple we become about "the way things are supposed to be." In learning how to survive when bad things happen to good people, how to carry on when we feel we have lost all that matters, and how to envision new horizons when the old ones dissolve, we become truly mature. We come to appreciate the paradoxes of life as the deepest reality of its mystery.

This is, I believe, the deepest ground of the perennial wisdom of our Catholic Christian faith. Our faith tells us that poor Lazarus winds up better off than the rich man, those who have all of life's successes and security may possibly be fools, and a "good thief" can steal heaven (Lk 16:19-31, 12:16-21, 23:39-43).

A radical incongruity in all this is that I am trying to articulate a basic truth of life's mystery and one of the basics of the mystery of our faith, yet this is precisely a mystery because it cannot fully be put into words! This realization has to make the insightful reader either laugh or cry! Laughing and crying together are, in my opinion, the touchstones of "worship in spirit and in truth" (Jn 4:24). Mutual support in the face of life's incongruities is, ultimately, all that really makes sense.

In the Dedication at the beginning of this book, I place love and laughter at the core of spirituality. Love and love alone can sustain the agony and the ecstasy of the paschal mystery. But the subtlety to which this leads is a glimpse of relativity in the common enterprise, or, if you will, the paradox of the mystery of the cross as a pledge of glory. When we recognize the incongruity and the paradox at the inner core of life's mystery, we must choose either to laugh or cry as our way of reaching out to others. The Christian, attuned to the gospel penchant for turning our world-view upside down, laughs—even, I believe, in the face of death.

While it may be nothing more than an ingrained bias inherited from my parents' way of viewing and experiencing life, I must confess that a sense of humor speaks to me of the mystery of God at the heart of the mystery of human life more than anything else. Since I believe that liturgy is where we most deliberately ritualize our spirituality, I have always attempted to integrate a sense of humor into my style of presiding at worship—not a corny playing on words or inane penchant for jokes but rather a sensitivity to the common ground of our humanity in coping with the mystery of life.

True wisdom is reserved in this life for that handful of people who can find an experience of God not only in the beauty of nature, the love of warm relationships and the integrity of peace and order, but also in the blank stares of anonymous faces in our nursing homes, or in the emptiness when one's last ray of hope is extinguished. Father Mike Jamail of Beaumont, Texas, says in some of his retreats that the real Christian is the one who can praise God from the ruins of life. The more I live the dregs and depths of life, the more I have come to believe in the "God of the unravelled," the God who is experienced not only when everything comes together but also when everything falls apart. For this is truly the God beyond the projection of our own fantasies, the God who is most truly Other. We begin by recognizing that our God is always enfleshed in human events and history—the immanent God. But coping with this incarnation inevitably leads us to encounter the transcendent God who is beyond, who is more than we can grasp.

My fourth and final insight is that we easily cope with a pluralism of spiritualities when we mature in the spiritual wisdom of the mystery of life. This wisdom cannot be captured by words. I hope the ones I am stringing together hint at it. I consider a person to be spiritual, that is, attuned to the Spirit of our God, to the extent that she or he is at home with the incongruities and paradoxes of this mystery of life, which implies being comfortable with the fact that there is no one right way of experiencing life.

In Conclusion

At this point, you might wonder if I am redefining the meaning of holiness. Yes! A pluralism of spiritualities is grounded in the fact that people are different from each other. A primary indicator of holiness is the ability to respect and accept that multifaceted created grace as something holy.

Openness to other ways of viewing and

experiencing life is the best sign of someone's degree of holiness and spiritual depth. Obviously, this implies an upheaval of the world-view of many church professionals— bishops, priests, religious, deacons and lay ministers. This upheaval may be the first real sign of their salvation. Using the criterion of sincere and genuine acceptance of others from whom we are truly different, in my experience the most holy and spiritual people I have ever met are usually categorized as the unchurched, the secular, the uneducated, and the worldly-wise bored with or indifferent to the ecclesiastical elite. The cleric who thinks he is God's incarnate grace has much to learn from the crusty old widow whose language makes him blush and whose horse-sense makes his erudite learning pale in comparison.

And so I conclude these chapters on the deeper meaning and implications of spirituality by directing the reader to the mystery of our daily lives. In the paradoxes and incongruities of an ordinary day we have the clearest window into the mystery of the God who is among us yet beyond us. Jesus blessed God for "hiding these things from the learned and the clever, and revealing them to mere children" (Mt 11:25). I suggest that those who know in their hearts what I am speaking about here are closest to the kingdom of God. How do you cope with a pluralism of spiritualities? The answer is discovered in the very process of becoming comfortable with life itself and its elusive mystery.

Epilogue

We stand on the threshold of a whole new world, a renewed church and a fresh spirituality. We are being re-shaped by the realization that mission is our identity. How we cope is increasingly an intuitive journey into the mystery of meaning. Something dramatic is starting to happen. Faith is becoming an experience of the breath of God in our face. The body and the spirit are contemplating marriage.

What I have written in the preceding pages is already past, a synthetic reflection upon where we've been. In a sense, much of what I have written here has become old hat. While I rationally affirm what you have long felt in your heart, you and I both sense that we have only just begun to glimpse the new horizons of our life in the Spirit. Even in our initial struggles to cope with pluralism, the wisdom and the challenge are grounded in the world of where we've been.

We still need a prophetic peek into the day after tomorrow. In my innermost heart, I see visions of a wildly different scenario based upon yet unspoken premises. Eye has not seen nor has ear heard, but hearts already know what is to come. Therefore, begging the reader's enjoyment of ambiguity, I want to close this book with a hint of further developments possible in our spirituality, let's say after the year 2010. What has been is prelude to what will be.

Agenda for the Day After Tomorrow:
—Imagine the Pieta. What does Mary, the Priest of the new creation, do after she finally lays to rest her Wounded Child?

—What earthy spirituality of the new age is emerging ever so gradually from the Mother-Waters of small faith sharing groups, both within and outside our parishes?

—What do the artists, the poets, the music composers, the playwrights and the novelists intuit about the world in the day after tomorrow?

—What dawning of the collective unconsciousness creeps into the sleepy dreams of spiritually sensitive individuals, dramatizing *our* rather than *my* unfolding story?

—How do you live in a world-view beyond the dichotomies of good and bad, right and wrong, conservative and liberal, old and new, sacred and secular, art and science, religion and culture, mysticism and technology, clergy and laity, gay and straight, order and chaos, feminine and masculine?

—What is the new heaven and the new earth, the small step/giant leap for humankind, when we, together at last, finally touch down on the big, blue-green marble?

—How do you know when to stop focusing the kaleidoscope?

On the third day, after we go into Galilee beyond the tomb, someone will rediscover Vatican II and come home to proclaim the kingdom of Jesus: Your crosses have become bridges to a second spring!

And on the eighth day there will be no more agenda. No "Amen!"

Notes

1   Cf. *The Seasons of a Man's Life*, Daniel
    J. Levinson, (Alfred A. Knopf, New York),
    1978; *Passages*, Gail Sheehy, (E.P.
    Dutton & Co., Inc., New York), 1974.

2   Cf. Henri J. Nouwen, *The Wounded
    Healer* (New York: Doubleday & Co.,
    1972); "Solitude and Contemporary
    Ministry: A Compassionate Ministry,"
    Sojourners, July 1980, pp. 18ff.

3   Henri Nouwen, "Solitude and
    Contemporary Ministry," *Sojourners*,
    June 1980, pp. 15-16.

4   Anne Wilson Schaef, *When Society
    Becomes An Addict* (San Francisco:
    Harper & Row, 1987).

5   Leonardo Boff, *Church: Charism &
    Power* (New York: Crossroad, 1986),
    pp. 65ff.

6   Matthew Fox, "A Pastoral Letter to
    Cardinal Ratzinger and the Whole
    Church," *Creation* (Vol. IV, No. 5,
    November/December, 1988, pp. 23-37).

7   Cf. Eugene Kennedy, *Tomorrow's
    Catholics/Yesterday's Church* (San
    Francisco: Harper & Row, 1988).

8   Karl Rahner, "Towards A Fundamental
    Theological Interpretation of Vatican II,"

Theological Studies (Georgetown University, 1979).

9   Cf. Richard McBrien, *Caesar's Coin: Religion and Politics in America,* (New York: Macmillan Press, 1987).

10   Riane Eisler, *The Chalice & the Blade* (San Francisco: Harper & Row, 1987).

11   For more about the psychic complexities involved, cf. Alice Miller, *The Drama of the Gifted Child* (New York: Basic Books, Inc., 1981).